Portraits

Elaine Feinstein is a poet, novelist and biographer. She has received many prizes, including a Cholmondeley Award for Poetry, Society of Authors', Wingate and Arts Council Awards, the Daisy Miller Prize for her experimental novel *The Circle* (longlisted for the 'lost' Man Booker Prize in 2010) and an honorary D.Litt. from the University of Leicester. She has travelled across the world to read her poems, and her books have been translated into most European languages, including Russian, as well as Chinese, Japanese and Korean. Her versions of the poems of Marina Tsvetaeva, a *New York Times* Book of the Year, have remained in print since 1971. She was given a major grant from Arts Council England to write her most recent novel, *The Russian Jerusalem* (Carcanet, 2008), a phantasmagoric mix of prose and poetry. She has served on the Council of the Royal Society of Literature, of which she is a Fellow, as a judge for most of the current literary prizes, and as chair of the judges for the T.S. Eliot Award. She received a Civil List Pension in 2010.

ELAINE FEINSTEIN

Portraits

CARCANET

First published in Great Britain in 2015 by
Carcanet Press Limited
Alliance House
Cross Street
Manchester M2 7AQ

www.carcanet.co.uk

A CIP catalogue record for this book is available from the British Library

ISBN 978 1 84777 215 2

The publisher acknowledges financial assistance from Arts Council England

Typeset by XL Publishing Services, Exmouth, UK

For Emma Tennant

Contents

Death and the Lemon Tree

Acknowledgements

Some of these poems have appeared in *Acumen, The Guardian, The Jewish Quarterly, The New Humanist, PN Review, Poem, Poetry London, Poetry Review, The Spectator,* and several anthologies, including *1914: Poetry Remembers* and *Jubilee Lines,* both edited by Carol Ann Duffy; also *A Mutual Friend: Poems for Charles Dickens,* edited by Peter Robinson. Earlier versions of six poems which clearly belonged in this book have appeared in other collections.

Portraits

Courting Danger

for Bella Akhmadulina

Those red sea urchins, Bella, on a platter of ice
alarmed me. Their spiky skins had to be
cracked open like chestnut cases, the creatures
still alive inside. Did I dare to broach them?
We were eating in Paris, somewhere near the Bastille.

You must have known that to dine with editors
from *Kontinent* was risky, but you'd spent
your life flirting with Soviet danger:
other writers lost pensions, ration cards, freedom
and some their lives for milder infringements

but mostly you avoided punishment,
and lived flamboyantly as Queen of Moscow.
In the West, émigré admirers bought champagne
and Sevruga caviar. These I shared greedily,
though your beauty made me dumb.

I could not ask if you still shook with a fever
that broke thermometers and appalled your neighbour,
or whether the gentle spirit of rain pursued you
into the houses of rich Party members
who urged you closer to the fire

as once a mob would have dragged you
into the flames as a witch. Perhaps that Yelabuga
you invented – whose eggs you threatened
to crush under your heels in payment
for Marina's death – took her own revenge

one day when her yellow eyes swivelled
towards you, hearing the tone of your laughter.
Or maybe she decided she could wait until,
many years later, she would find you
sick and blind, and could move in for the kill.

April Fools' Day

i.m. Isaac Rosenberg (1890–1918)

Does anybody know what it was all for?
Not Private Rosenberg, short as John Keats.
A nudge from Ezra Pound took him to war,
to sleep on boards, in France, with rotting feet,
writing his poetry by candle ends.
His fellow soldiers always found him odd.
Outsiders do not easily make friends,
if they are awkward – with a foreign God.

He should have stayed in Cape Town with his sister.
Did he miss Marsh's breakfasts at Gray's Inn,
or Café Royal? He longed for the centre
though he was always shy with Oxbridge toffs –
he lacked the sexy eyes of Mark Gertler –
and his *Litvak* underlip could put them off.
'*From Stepney East!*' as Pound wrote
Harriet Monroe, while sending poems to her.

He died on April Fools' Day on patrol.
beyond the corpses lying in the mud,
carrying up the line a barbed wire roll
– useless against gunfire – with the blood
and flesh of Death in the spring air.
His was the life half lived, if even that,
and the remains of it were never found. We remember:
the iron honey gold, his cosmopolitan rat.

Life Class: A Sketch

In Paris, perhaps. On wet cobbles,
walking alone at night, fragile
and wispily dressed, Jean Rhys,
without a *sou*, past streets
of lit cafés to a meeting place.

Cold to the bone, she has it all planned:
when they go home, she'll fall
at his knees, gaze up like a child,
and make him understand
he cannot abandon her,

lost in a strange land.
His grey eyes are indifferent as
the North Sea to her need –
if she tries to plead
her words will drown.

So she smiles instead.
That's how she'll cope with crooks
and pick-ups, drink and veronal
in those grim boarding houses
that now stretch ahead.

Over and over she will write the story
of frail girls and the unkindness of men,
speaking in the voice of her cool notebooks,
until one day a frightened Creole self
climbs down from the attic of memory

in the shape of the first Mrs Rochester,
betrayed, barefoot, imprisoned
in an England of snow and roses,
constrained in Thornfield Hall, a dangerous
ghost – that apparition brings success.

Jean entertains in a Knightsbridge hotel,
elegant in her seventies to meet her fame,
with eyes like dark blue pools:
'Too late,' she says, 'Too late', without irony,
as her looks fade – into a ninth decade.

Emanuel

i.m. Emanuel Litvinoff (1915–2011)

With your sardonic, Sam Spade elegance,
the pale clothes always clean and pressed,
and that lean body women knew at once
would give them pleasure, still, those bitter
lines from nose to mouth suggest
you felt a sense of failure,

a childhood misery always ready to pounce,
from the doorways you slept in, long ago.
Writing saved you once,
and books in the Whitechapel library:
A poet, like the Messiah, carries no cash.
You were precociously aware of poetry;

wrote soldier-lyrics, then, after the war
found the Cosmo, and Canetti.
An angry poem at the ICA
in the voice of a Bleistein relative
made you notorious, all the more
since Eliot himself sat in the audience.

Your theme was waiting. Wandering off from your
chic wife's catwalk into Moscow's 'Thaw',
you found disabled creatures from the Gulag
who told their stories in familiar Yiddish,
the *lingua franca* of the twentieth century.
It became your mission to portray

their Europe in your novels, while beneath
the desk, scuffed carpet showed the wriggling
of feet forever longing to walk free –
until evening entered the room as street light,
releasing you from that prose duty
into the living world of Mecklenburgh Square.

The Gamble

i.m. Sylvia Plath (1932–1963)

The woman in the mirror swimming
towards you like a terrible fish
never made landfall. Look upon this fin.
Observe the lines the scars the teeth the skin.
I am old as you will never be.

Your life was shorter than Mozart's or Pushkin's.
I remember living through the humiliation
you were too proud to bear, and now to imagine
the motive for your dying troubles me – was it
your poems that demanded that last gesture?

I honour your carbon-paper skies
typed through with stars, those winter trees
dissolving in their blotting-paper clouds.
You threw away the last half century
as if your death could be a deal you cut

with genius, in return for fame
and those ferocious poems, blossoming
in the unnatural freeze of '63.
Was it your legend that demanded blood
to prove the violence packed in every lyric

was no pretence? Sadly, it was authentic.
You could have had the man back in your bed
if you'd been willing to endure suspicion. Was hatred
cleaner, did you prefer to damage him
when he saw your healthy body dead?

What if the doctor's number had been found
and you had woken up to Ted's embrace –
seen his remorse – would a new life begin,
would brushing death have kept him safely bound,
was that the happy end you fell asleep in?

Do not rise up now with your red hair
to mock an audience which has come to stare
at the fairground Lady in your story;
explain instead what gamble made you waste
your energy and grace – and the taste of glory.

Homesickness

i.m. Maria Fadeyeva Enzensberger (1943–1991)

Yesterday I found a postcard with your scrawl:
'Darling, we are all horses, how is it
you haven't learned that yet?' And at once
your high-boned, white face rose
beside me like a reproach

as if I had begun to forget the wildness
in the gutturals of your laugh, and
the loneliness of *tosca po rodine*
in the frozen sea of your eyes. But I have not.
You were always my Russia:

the voice of Marina's poetry. We saw you last
in a Moscow of brown streets, puddles, and
people queuing for ice cream: an autumn of anomalies,
women turning back tanks, in St Petersburg
there were teenage boys playing *Deutschland über alles*.

Your mother, the poet Aliger, brought us into
Sologub's yellow mansion where Ivan found himself
in his underpants and writers fix their *dachas*:
Bulgakov would have enjoyed the chicken livers in coriander.
That day you were shaking with the euphoria

of street victory, as if you had come home
after the bleakness that took you into
Highgate hospital. 'I have been so *frightened*,'
you whispered to me there and I had no answer,
any more than at your table in the Cambridge fens

rich with forest mushrooms, peppers and white cheese,
when you struck the glass to command some speech
of love and closeness, and we all failed you. In London
you found another silence, and now we're only left with
a little honey and sun from Mandelstam's dead bees.

Dickens Considers Fagin

'Let me break up the lines.
                There's moonlight now.
Wet London cobbles. Shadows,
                the stink of frying onions.
Red-haired, in raggy night gear,
                a merry old gentleman
offers friendship, sausages, hot gin
                to his pack of street children:
his family workshop's warmer
                than the workhouse.

"My dear," he croons, "my dear,"
                and soon that voice is in my ears,
he is given life, he's loose
                in my imagination,
I let him tap into centuries
                of thieving peddlers.
Cruikshank gave him a woolly caftan
                cross-hatched for texture,
stood him by the fire with a toasting fork,
                like the devil, though I remember
thinking – Bill Sikes is more brutal.

As I had Fagin cower in his cell, waiting to be
                hanged, I was puzzled, though:
how did I hit on the name? – Irish, not Ashkenazi,
                and Bob Fagin was kind to me long ago
in the blacking factory. The choice
                was part of a writer's game,
which has its own rules of vitality,
                as much as the gestures of caricature;
no wakeful effort to correct the damage
                by drawing Riah can begin to cure.'

The Irony of Wisława Szymborska

In London, I remember the indignation.
    Surely the Nobel prize should have gone
to Zbigniew Herbert, the Polish poet we loved
    – dissident, charismatic, much translated –
not some woman we had barely heard of?

I thought Polish poems should resemble films of Wajda,
    charged with the electricity of war.
Szymborska's poetry held no such glamour.
    She had not played a part in the Resistance.
The poems were almost English in their texture,

a bit like Larkin – though serene
    where he was glum – never
expecting to fill a football stadium.
    Her voice was quieter than Cassandra's –
but equally we did not listen to her.

Her vision lay in refusing to make patterns
    out of the casual happenstance of fortune
– who survives a massacre, who marries again.
    Of life's mistakes, she only murmurs sadly
This particular course is never offered twice.

Luftmensch

i.m. Joseph Roth (1894–1939)

After *Radetzky March* and world success,
      he had to learn – since Nazis
blocked his German publication –
      to live on the run
between cities – Cologne, Antibes,
      Leipzig, Paris – pursued
by creditors, hustling for advances.

In photographs his eyes remain amused,
      the cheekbones high.
Fearless and feckless,
      he still enjoyed Grand Hotels,
rich dinners and champagne,
      with the novelist Irma Keun
a lovely companion.

Disreputable charmer, he found patrons –
      distinguished writer friends,
like Stefan Zweig in Mexico –
      but gambled away his gains.
How could that matter once
      the catastrophe he prophesied
was round him? As he wrote: *Hell reigns.*

Luftmensch and wanderer, he hedged
      his last bet: two funerals, one
Jewish, one Catholic. A witty entry
      into the next world. Genius
is a changeling, registered in no parish:
      'I'm always at home,' he said
'Wherever I feel unhappy.'

Dizzy in Westminster

Glossy black ringlets, blistering waistcoats, silver-buckled shoes.
Where did you get the nerve for such flamboyance?
Not from your father, skull-capped and scholarly,
whose anger with his Synagogue released you
into the gentile world, a baptised Jew.

Always in debt, and eager for renown, only
literary fame and a witty tongue gave you
entry to river parties and heady dinners
where politicians ate swan stuffed with truffles
and married women readily became your tutors.

How did you bewitch those stolid gentlemen
of the shires to choose you for a leader?
Baptism did not make you less a Jew,
cartoonists mocked your aquiline profile
and drooping lip. Parliament was your theatre.

Gladstone thought your talent opportunist,
disliked your eloquence, and found you slippery.
Let us confess your policy Imperialist,
your shrewdest foreign deals somehow
congruent with your own extravagance.

Yet courage trumps all and demands tribute.
You flattered, entertained, but never cringed.
And that, dear Earl of Beaconsfield, I salute.

A Charred Slipper

i.m. Zelda Fitzgerald (1900–1948)

A flash of dazzling hair and the gaiety
    of a wide, unsteady smile:
she glows in the sunlight of his success,

his writing suffused with her presence.
    An enviable marriage,
with Paris always shimmering around them.

She could have basked in his splendour
    for life, but was it sickness
to need something of her own? Doctors ruled out ballet.

Jazz, alcohol, dancing, celebrity
    left her waking into self-hatred;
her notebooks held the world she could be making.

Why did Scott write to Scribner's to advise
    she should not be given praise,
being too unstable for superlatives?

After publication, the petering out of hope.
    More doctors, misery, hospitals,
her fragile intelligence fed letters and diaries

he used tenderly in his own novels.
    Well, he paid the bills,
while she pined away in nursing homes

a reluctant Muse, hating to be consumed.
    Her unused talent
flickered while she lived, until

her beauty went up in flames in Carolina.
    When she was dead, only
one charred slipper remained under her bed.

Sleepless Nights

Outside: a rain-splintered table
        streaked with lavender,
a magpie pecking in the stone pot
        where each summer
stems rise in green desire
        to be fists of agapanthus.
Six a.m. I have lost a night
        as Elizabeth Hardwick's reader –

remembering my own husband
        shambling to bed:
those tirades of hammering words,
        and being shaken awake
again and then again,
        my heart out of rhythm.
It is not easy to share a bed with
        an unhappy man.

Lowell had form. His three wives knew
        the rage beneath the poetry,
the violence under the charm:
        Boston Brahmin –
Cal from his schooldays, both
        Caligula and Caliban.
His women learned the pattern:
        faithless highs – sad equilibrium.

Was he going back to Elizabeth
        when he died in the New York cab?
I met his Lady Caroline,
        over lunch in Notting Hill:
a little drunk, with a queenly drawl,
        and her eyes still
large enough to drown in.

Dreaming Raymond Chandler

Strange now to think of you wanting to live in La Jolla,
      with Cissy old and sick,
tired of LA, bent cops and the vernacular
      you made into a poetry for Bogart.

Why would you long for that posh suburb, I wonder?
      I lived there for a time, close by the cliffs
of San Diego, where hang-gliders ride
      on thermal gusts above the Pacific ocean,

nowhere more remote from my war-time dream
      of your LA as sexy, and far darker
than the Cotton Club and fashionable
      nights in Harlem.

I wanted to slink through your books
      in elegant shoes
and cool beige clothes, always belted in tightly –
      as if I had nothing to lose,

or else be a private dick myself in a fedora,
      living among thugs,
enduring pain for pay – enjoying drink,
      despising other drugs.

Marlowe was your invention. You were mine.
      I fell for your underworld
of *film noir* streets and ice-cool banter.
      In fact, you were bemused by Billy Wilder,

being a pupil of Dulwich College for a time
      and a mother's boy, who was
mainly loyal to an ageing wife. Your dreams
      leaked into mine – the first trick of a writer!

Marina's Ghost Visits Akhmatova

Our shadows live for ever
— Anna Akhmatova

As Anna dreams, her profile sharp
        as if struck on a coin, Marina is
trudging through frozen mud,
        to the plank over a slope,
a village hut, the nail, a hank of rope…

Anna wakes, her heartbeat uneven,
        warm air against her skin,
in Tashkent where carnations smell of Asia,
        far south from her own
city of water and starvation.

She feels for an old gown — Chinese silk
        embroidered with a dragon,
the seam torn but no matter — trying to think
        only of the world around her:
vodka, peaches, handsome Polish officers,

but she cannot shrug off the shadow
        or her knowledge of
a great poet's death alone.
        She looks over the edge
into the blackness of a final departure,

never guessing she will survive
        another generation of murders,
be surprised by late honours
        and that her last hospital bed
is distant by a quarter century.

A Yorkshireman in Provence

i.m. Anthony Ward, novelist (1937–1994)

It was February in Provence and the local market
sold goats' cheese wrapped in chestnut leaves and
thick, painted pottery. The stalls of dark check shirts
were the kind you used to wear, and we began to see you:
burly, bearded, handsome as Holbein's Wyatt,
looking into the eyes of a girl or
jumping up from the brasserie table
to buy truffles from a street vendor.

We stayed with our children like gypsies in a barn
of your wife's family house near Aix, and you fed us
beef *daube*, thrush pâté and wine. Long ago
we sat through the night as a threesome writing
those film reviews I always drove to Heffers
in the early rainlight of a Cambridge morning. We still own
the pearwood Dolmetsch bought at your urging,
and copies of that magazine you and I ran together

which the police came to investigate after
a delivery of *Naked Lunch* from Olympia.
For a few years, you moved whenever we did,
from Adams Road to Sherlock, then De Freville
where the printer we owed money lived next door.
You wrote your first book for three hours a day
and then felt restless, since your body liked
to use its energies and you could lift a car.

Your hair was thick and brown
even in York District Hospital where you murmured
'I'm not dying, am I?' and described
the wild animals calmed with a click in your throat.
We guessed you could withstand a February *mistral*
that gets under the clothes so bitterly down here
more easily than we did, being younger
and more robust though, strangely, no longer alive.

Siegfried Sassoon and the Wish to Belong

Behind his father's name lay the whole landscape
    of Baghdad's palaces and *souks*
with smells and tastes and spices
    unknown to England's gentle country folk.
Old money, but a father disinherited
    for marrying outside the Jewish family.
When he was four, his parents separated.
    His father died soon after of TB.

The Christian name? His Anglo-Catholic mother
    chose that for love of Wagner's operas.
If Siegfried felt little connection with
    scruffy refugees in flight from Tsars
he learned early to dislike much more
    the show of wealth in merchant relatives.
Aside from figures of the Old Testament
    he found his ancestry an embarrassment.

Not a bad start, though: Marlborough,
    Clare College, modest private income,
and turning out a decent cricketer.
    When war came, he enlisted as an officer.
Once on the Western Front, he made
    so many single-handed 'mad Jack' raids,
carrying back the English wounded,
    his courage won him the Military Cross.

As poet, wittiest of his generation,
    he wrote of war as only soldiers know it:
old buffers joking cheerfully with men
    soon *done for* with a flawed plan of attack;
a placid woman, knitting socks, and chatting
    even as, over there, the line falls back
and her son's face is trodden into mud.

That letter against the war, read out in Parliament,
        was treated not as treason, but as illness.
A hero, he was sent away for treatment.
        first hospital, then sunny Palestine,
surviving into the world between two wars,
        grieving for lost friends but loving
other men: Ivor Novello, Stephen Tennant.
        He even married, had a son.

Fortunate, then. He chose assimilation –
        into an English literary life,
friendships among artists and aristocrats
        indulgent towards sexual adventure,
whatever other prejudice they had.
        He never lost a Jewish need for God,
joining the Roman Catholic Church at seventy.
        He wanted to belong, not to be free.

The Marriage of Thomas and Jane Carlyle

*It was very good of God to let Carlyle and Mrs Carlyle marry one another and
so make only two people miserable and not four*

– Samuel Butler

He fell in love at once. Not Jane,
who was more taken with his stylish friend.
A pretty girl, ready to flirt with suitors,
she had to ignore his clumsiness, dyspepsia,
the local accent he refused to lose,
and (for all the wit) uncertain future.

Never pretending to be in love with him,
she grew dependent on their conversation,
agreed to an engagement, blew hot and cold
(they both did) and at length agreed to marriage.
Such a great friendship they might have enjoyed
if they had not begun to share a household.

A frugal life, even after *The French Revolution*
brought the great world to Cheyne Row.
Did they even try sleeping together?
There were no children. Both were often ill
– and Jane recovered best away from home.
Strangely, apart, their letters could be tender,

Jane wrote to him of *comforting with kisses* –
confessing she knew they'd row once back together.
With guests, her voice was always strong as his;
she liked to make fun of his grumpiness
in front of a shocked, attentive audience.
And young men were infatuated by her presence.

Most of what Thomas wanted he achieved:
admirers, world recognition, a sufficiency.
Her gifts began to fade compared to his:
the dancing girl with her long eyelashes
he barely noticed now. Her letters fizzed
with the shrewd details of a novelist

but something held her back from such a risk –
while he paid homage to his Lady Ashburton
for *cheerfulness* he could not find at home.
Morphine and sleeplessness then took their toll.
In the Tait photograph of the Carlyles
her skin looks shrivelled, eyes no longer bold.

Carlyle retreated to a soundproofed room.
Jane felt unwanted, frequently sustained
only by women friends she entertained –
with *vignettes* of grim days – to her last breath.
She would not have been much consoled to witness
the depth of his remorse after her death.

Dr Who in Las Vegas

This is planet Nevada, an old spring
     in the Mohave desert, once the outpost
of Mob and Rat Pack, each hotel
     now a toy town. Look,
the *Venice* has canals for gondoliers,
     a mock-up of St Mark's has a fake sky
to hold in savage air-conditioning.

Outside the bubble, day heat is 106.
     The car lights along the strip at night
glow white as electric fish.
     In the lobby, Daleks jiggle and flash;
a worshipper, with slippers on her feet,
     feeds one her last cash.
What do I find in this city of games

with dead men in the desert and
     the Tardis waiting to manifest solidity?
America itself, the *goldene medina*,
     a land of plenty, just a moment more,
until real power shifts across to Asia.
     Bring on the Doctor, then, though I hesitate
to put my money on the River Card.

The Generation of Gabriela Mistral

Ships carry away the ones we love
Along the white road they are taken away...
— Marina Tsvetaeva

As if a meteor had struck the planet
    releasing some inner energy:
a whole generation of women
    began to write poetry,

from the *Stray Dog* in St Petersburg
    to the outback of Chile.
And one of them, a fatherless child,
    made her mark on history.

Her pseudonym was redolent
    of an angel and Provence –
and the people loved her songs. She was
    politician and saint at once.

She was sent to Madrid as attaché
    in a time of civil war;
she pitied the face of refugees,
    and hated fascist law.

She had to lose the woman she loved
    and the boy she counted her son
to write in madness out of loss –
    the ancient lament of women.

Flair

That whole wet summer, I listened to Louis Armstrong.
Imagined him arriving in New York after Funky Butt
dance halls, wearing hick clothes: those
high-top shoes with hooks, and long
underwear down to his socks.

Thought of him shy in a slick, new band, locked
for two weeks reading the part he was set,
until the night when Bailey on clarinet
took over an old song. Then Louis' horn
rose in harsh, elated notes,

phrases he'd invented on riverboats
and ratty blues tonks, using all the sinews
of his face and muscle of his tongue.
And what delights me now
is when he grinned to thank

the crowd that stood to clap, he saw
slyly from the corner of his eye
all the stingy players in the band
were sitting motionless, their tribute
only an astonished sigh.

Down and Out

i.m. Bessie Smith (1894–1937)

Huge in wig and feathers, your bold stance
      declares a Chattanooga
childhood of street fights, alcohol and poverty –
      so how, on long-haul drives,
can I pretend to share in your defiance?

And yet your song of triumph fills my throat.
      Together, we assert female
demands against the tyranny of men,
      and rise above the fear of loneliness,
as if we were both somehow in the same boat

– even though I am a skinny white woman
      while you are black and tough –
because we loved the same kind of man.
      Your voice will keep me sane.
If I ever get on my feet again…

A Young Wife Listens to Piaf

The pin is loose that holds the climbing rose.
         It crackles on the glass. I stare outside
at a single wet goat with oblong eyes:
         bemused – a young wife and mother,
beyond the Gogs – and my own story over.

Family clothes are not yet folded away,
         the children are watching some illicit TV,
up here, a piercing voice from the radio
         has begun to reach deeply into me:
Edith Piaf, and the songs she chose

of failed loves, loneliness, poverty.
         Suddenly, I long for her Paris streets,
and the glamour of a woman
         who never had safety to lose –
the thin child with a monstrous voice

rattling centimes in a hat – those walls of mirrors
         in grand restaurants, the Dietrich eyebrows,
even the drug pallor. All of it was her choice,
         a tiny woman in a black dress,
with an audience ready to watch her collapse on stage

Rien, je ne regrette rien. While I, in bland
         everyday disorder, listen
to the soaring triumph in her voice, knowing
         she has only earned that elation, because
she learned to sell her ordinary life for applause.

Billie Holiday in Chalcot Gardens

i.m. Billie Holiday (1915–1959)

Lady Day, I never saw you on 52nd Street
      with a gardenia in your hair,
and your black eyes empty, as if heroin
      had scraped away the horrors
inside your head, leaving your spirit bare.

You sang on vinyl in our living room
      level with sycamore trees
of brutal police and miserable loves,
      warding off the pain with gestures
in white, silk-jersey gloves.

You knew the night. Yes, that was where you lived
      those poisonous highs
in the circle of the spotlight, hardly moving –
      your voice seems to break
on the word *unhappy* in surprise.

A phantom took the applause
      you did not need.
The music already carried you towards
      the somewhere else
you set off for bravely, in your lynx fur,

some predatory young hood in tow
      – smoking, drinking, using
whatever drug dispelled your gloom –
      any memories left dispersed
in your pink-satin bedroom.

Your glittering presence was no comfort to me.
      I was too much afraid
of the reality your voice brought in
      and the lonely truths
of that last darkness none of us has made.

The Undercover Rider

i.m. R.B. Kitaj (1932–2007) and Isaac Babel (1894–1940)

A swirl of ochre – then a brighter yellow
fills in the woodcut lines of an alien figure;
another stubby man wears a red scarf:
carnival colours. What's the story here?

This is the euphoria of revolution:
Ukraine in flames, the air a grey smoke.
Ash beneath dark skies. From a horse's white rump,
the colours turn in a kaleidoscope.

But where is Babel? Such insolence
for a myopic Jew – to ride
alongside Kuban Cossacks into Chagall's
villages of dirt-floor shacks.

The Whites have already trashed the *shtetl.*
Babel rides with the Red Cavalry,
shamed by their courage, though they loot and kill.
Bystander angel, he records the dying.

Kitaj has sketched a man with a bird's head,
against the scribbled map of a little town,
an image styled after a medieval
haggadah, telling the story of Passover.

Secrets of a shared family tree:
the faithful passions of the trapped,
the cheating promises of liberty –
Kitaj, like Babel, draws the savagery.

Burning Bright

for Valentina

Your hair is streaked with carrot and henna,
       your green eyes – feline jewels:
in furs, you resemble a Siberian tiger,

or else a witch. You flew to Moscow once –
       your broomstick only the metal ledge
outside a train – leaving that prisoners' village

where nobody wanted you as a child.
       A descendant of Poles,
you were too bookish and too wild.

So you ran away – what did you have to lose?
       Unscared of strangeness,
in Moscow you fell in with clever Jews

who helped you find your way – university,
       out of Russia, Africa. Today,
hearing English slurs, you still defend us boldly.

This comes to thank you for your nerve:
       hassling princes and prelates equally
to have good poets helped as they deserve

while loving your sick husband tenderly.
       Should I have brought you
Ferrero Rocher or pink champagne,

an agate ring, a string of fragrant bay?
       No. All you need is to inspire
writers you cherish – in the name of Brodsky.

Old Muse

Do you remember when you dreamed
of T.S. Eliot and a chestnut stallion
bundled into a taxi? The Old Possum
spectacled, a little furtive, the animal
glowing, both dismissed together

as if from your own life. The vision
disturbed you, as if it were a sign
that imagination itself might be
dwindling away. Not so, old friend.
Your spirit is the living stuff of poetry

as it was that first winter in Wiltshire,
when we walked together beneath wet trees,
past a black stub alder, the roots gashed
with witches' fungus, frosty leaves
crackling under our feet.

We spoke of obdurate women who fought
to become themselves, listened to cries
of mallard across the marshes, shared
a drunken glee, even though I was scared
by the natural sorcery of the forest.

Over the years you conjured poems
from my sad thoughts and with your laughter
taught me how to shrink snubs and disasters,
so that even now I recognise your power.
I won't deny there have been silences,

more than the usual drifting away in age.
No matter now for that. I'm sad you've lost
your stride and sailing carriage,
but it was the inner fire in you I loved
and that still burns: indomitable courage.

Immortal in Kensal Rise

Shadows press in tonight
      among the laughter and talk
at a dinner table by candlelight,
      all of us patched up
after anaesthetic and surgery –
      our generations' trenches.
We exchange the names of the fallen
      with the shudder of survivors.

Their past work stands around us
      without reproach, but sadly,
along the maple bookshelves.
      We search the spines and wonder
how long their songs and stories
      will survive in a digital age.
Will the young still come across them
      without a physical page?
And then perforce remember
      where we shall rest ourselves.

Voice

for Tony Rudolf

If not now, when?
                    – Hillel

Is it shyness, childhood doubts, or
            giving too much reverence
to those you admire, has made you squander
            for so long your prodigious energies
on a tireless advocacy of others?

In publishing, in praising, in translation,
            you introduce one mind to another
and they love you casually, maybe observing
            the slate blue of your eyes
and your slim fitness, but still looking past you

as you seem to prefer, and even though
            you are altogether seen,
every plane of your flesh recorded
            in paint by a great artist,
your own inventions still wait to be written

and you should understand: we want
            your voice as it is on the telephone,
humanly observant, intriguing us
            with unexpected juxtapositions.
Risk it, old friend. Write poems now. Or your own fictions.

On Not Dying Young

In blinding sunlight on streets wet with rain
          I brought my first son home
into our shabby flat near Free School Lane.

It was Cambridge weather: late February,
          a cold wind at the sill,
and shillings needed for the gas meter.

You were fixing the radio, preoccupied
          with plugs and trailing wires.
I let my body feed our sturdy child.

When was it, maybe ten days later?
          that sudden flood of red –
a lake of blood on the bathroom floor,

then a stretcher under the stars, and voices:
          'The idiots left a swab inside her.'
'Will she live?' I counted down to four:

Death hath ten thousand several doors
          I would not enter.
Waking, my left arm was strapped to a board.

They brought my baby to me when he cried,
          I was too weak to hold him,
but my milk still flowed. And you were there,

whispering, while I drowsed, breathing in
          the newly unfamiliar scent
of that wild flower – life.

Self-Portrait in the Olympic Summer

This August is mainly silence. No travel abroad, no garden party,
only a quiet working day with time for thought and books.

Trouble is, once the pressure is off, the hours
go past me, clear as running water.

Across the city, people are cheering athletes,
while the West End is eerily quiet. Empty.

Summer has been cancelled this year, it seems.
No fruit to ripen. My soggy garden rots.

Black windows look into wet rosemary. Yes,
when the phone is silent, I feel my loneliness.

St Lucy's Day

for J.H.

We are halfway through the dark time.
        They know it in their roots, the winter trees:
while I sit brooding over the keys,

out there in the garden, snow coming on,
        they need no plan to blossom and seed –
the earth provides for their time to come.

If words could rise as simply, I should sing
        of the power – never to be proved or shaken –
whose silence answers human aspiration.

The name of the man who invented the wheel
        has been forgotten,
along with his language, his gods, his stories.

Where are his bones,
        his tombstone?
                Who has seen his ghost?

An Oxford Beauty

Soaked from a rainstorm, shivering
        in the ladies' lavatory of Balliol,
I found a woman twenty years younger
        staring hard into the same mirror,
pulling back strands of wet, pale hair
        into the teeth of two silver clips.

With her full mouth, fine bones, lean face,
        she was serenely beautiful. She whispered:
'The skies outside are dark as the Apocalypse,
        and, for myself, I wouldn't much care
if today were the end of the universe.'

What caused her such extravagant distress?
        I did not ask, but guessed,
for lovely women, more ruthless than others,
        are reckless, too, which is why
they make the best spies, being as ready
        to throw their lives away as meet a lover.

A Video of Habima at the Globe (2012)

How elegant the discipline of your shapes,
  the line of the dance, the twang
of those exotic instruments:
  such gaiety, such impudence,
invented through a perilous history
  from Białystok to Stalin's Moscow.

Here you are in London for a festival
  of Shakespeare transmuted, say,
into Urdu or Chinese. Can his plays live
  using the guttural
language of the Hebrew Bible?
  Your leaving Russia led to Tel Aviv.

That move explains these flags, loud music,
  watchful police.
That's why we pass through airport security,
  and so many people pack into the lobby.
A strip of land, hard-won by refugees
  has stirred the anger of new enemies.

Adrenalin flows in the blood as the crowd
  are allowed in to find their own seats –
we have been warned there will be interruptions.
  The play is *The Merchant of Venice*,
and these performers open with a mime
  of three louts bullying an old man.

Shouts rise as Shylock pleads *Do we not bleed?*
  but quietly protesters are led outside.
No bombs are thrown. The wiry troupe proceed
  and the audience maybe warms toward
their nerve, the irony they give the story –
  at the end some stand up to applaud.

The actors bow their thanks, except for one:
        Shylock, a defeated man, alone,
walks off-stage through the auditorium,
        a single battered suitcase in his hand.
Will he find peace in the Middle East?
        Borders flame around the longed-for homeland.

Love

Some enchantment kept me moving once
between two monsters and I loved them both,
delighted by the shameless urgency
of their demands, their needy certainties,
cajoled, instructed, often damaged most
by my own insensate wish to please.

A bold woman, and a man without mercy.
How could I withstand such intense presence?
Scholars, like housekeepers, have their own domain
and might perhaps have put up some resistance
but what does any poet know deeply enough,
other than an inner world of shadows?

There will be a gale tonight: October again.
A few leaves already blow in the gutter.
I speak frankly in a rare moment
of purity after those years ill-spent:
both of you were more unhappy than I was.
It would be inappropriate to complain.

My Polish Cleaner's Version

'A puzzle, this old woman in her nightie
standing at a computer before breakfast.

What is she doing so urgently while
yesterday's dishes are still in the sink,

books scattered over the living-room floor?
She is working, she explains. She is a writer.

I don't read much myself – my English is bad –
but some of the books have her name on the cover.

One day, she gave me a translation into Polish
of a book she had written about a Russian poet.

I hate Russia and I never liked poetry.
Still, it would not have been polite to refuse.

In Poland, I was taught Jews were careful with money
but this one leaves hers in small change everywhere,

and when she doesn't have enough to pay me
we gather what we can together and she laughs,

apologising for the weight of the coins. I tell her:
'All of it is money!'   She is like a child.

These days, when I am ready to go, I say
'Take a rest over the weekend!' And she agrees

without listening, already lost in the screen.
And I understand now. *What she does there is her life.*'

Death and the Lemon Tree

Death and the Lemon Tree

1

My foolish indoor tree, this sudden exuberance
        of sweet-smelling flowers troubles me.
Surely it is reckless, when your leaves have been falling
        ever since you were put in the new pot?
Somewhere in your helical code the instructions
        have been fucked up.

Last year I picked your fruit with reverence,
        taking pride in the full flesh.
Today as I feed your roots the intense
        blue crystals for citrus fruit
your heady perfume is no longer rich
        as the low notes of a flute.

Bare wood. Scuffed petals. No question,
        you are under stress.
How can I heal you? More water? Less?
        This is a peculiar season.
I don't even know if it is snow outside the glass

or white blossom torn from the late cherry.
        No matter, for a grey-eyed friend
has taken garden shears to my sick tree,
        and boldly snipped the boughs
saying, 'the roots will search under the soil and spread'.
        Unless, I thought, they are dead.

2

Tinsel hopes. Cold dreams. A year
of ghosts, and the drift of gravel,

away from the shore, the tide between my toes
and no hold against the pull of the sea.

Too many friends are gone, from every
page of my life, and there is even

something treacherous in me, almost
consenting to the whisper of a gentle voice

saying – *weaker by the day, but not in pain,*
and reconciled to dying – sooner rather than later –

Those last words undermine me:
not as a temptation, more

a sudden snuffing out of urgency,
for where is the sense of all this focus

in a rainy June of late-night radio
and mornings spent looking through glass

at a garden of overgrown bushes
and grass too wet to mow. Downhill –

so why not simply coast? It's not my way.
Work is my game. It's how I play.

3

And I shall keep my date to read in Greece –
        Athens in crisis, riots in the Plaka,
but also sunshine, poetry, Mount Parnassus,
        ancient names beckon.

Although in Delphi there is no oracle,
        no cave of murmurs,
in the ruins of Apollo's temple,
        behind broken columns

too heavy for looters, I can hear
        the tread of a history
old as Jerusalem
        and still numinous.

The god himself has vanished
        as if no-one ever brought
goats and treasure into his sanctuary
        to beg his healing power.

What the looters missed the Church destroyed.
        Only black basalt of the mountainside
reminds us of Zeus and earthquake,
        stories of a people

old as my own, both seductive
        and a danger to each other.
Their troubles. Our troubles.
        Equally brutal.

On the way back to Athens:
        hillsides of lemon trees
Persian traders brought here from Asia
        along the Silk Road.

They flourish in terraces,
        their progeny immortal
even when neglected,
        surviving centuries.

4

Home again, and what's this? Three or four delicate tips
with a pinky sheen have broken
the grey skin of the lemon branches.
Can these be new leaves?
I am not imagining them. There has been
a vegetable resurrection
in my absence. So, you're not finished yet,
my resilient tree. Good. Let us age further.